JIM ARNOSKY

At This Very Moment

Dutton Children's Books • An imprint of Penguin Group (USA) Inc.

JIM ARNOSKY

At This Very Moment

Dutton Children's Books • *An imprint of Penguin Group (USA) Inc.*

For Tom and Natalie

Dutton Children's Books
A division of Penguin Young Readers Group

Published by the Penguin Group
Penguin Group (USA) Inc., 375 Hudson Street, New York, New York 10014, U.S.A.
Penguin Group (Canada), 90 Eglinton Avenue East, Suite 700, Toronto, Ontario M4P 2Y3, Canada
(a division of Pearson Penguin Canada Inc.)
Penguin Books Ltd, 80 Strand, London WC2R 0RL, England
Penguin Ireland, 25 St Stephen's Green, Dublin 2, Ireland (a division of Penguin Books Ltd)
Penguin Group (Australia), 250 Camberwell Road, Camberwell, Victoria 3124, Australia
(a division of Pearson Australia Group Pty Ltd)
Penguin Books India Pvt Ltd, 11 Community Centre, Panchsheel Park, New Delhi - 110 017, India
Penguin Group (NZ), 67 Apollo Drive, Rosedale, North Shore 0632, New Zealand
(a division of Pearson New Zealand Ltd)
Penguin Books (South Africa) (Pty) Ltd, 24 Sturdee Avenue, Rosebank, Johannesburg 2196, South Africa
Penguin Books Ltd, Registered Offices: 80 Strand, London WC2R 0RL, England

Library of Congress Cataloging-in-Publication Data
Arnosky, Jim.
At This Very Moment/ by Jim Arnosky. — 1st ed.
p. cm.
ISBN 978-0-525-42252-5 (hardcover)
Special Markets ISBN 978-0-525-42595-3 Not for resale
[1. Stories in rhyme. 2. Nature—Fiction. 3. Animals—
Habits and behavior—Fiction.] I. Title.
PZ8.3.A648At 2011 [E]—dc22 2010037711

Manufactured in China by Dutton Children's Books,
a division of Penguin Young Readers Group
345 Hudson Street, New York, New York 10014
www.penguin.com/youngreaders

Designed by Abby Kuperstock

Manufactured in China
10 9 8 7 6 5 4 3 2 1

This Imagination Library edition is published by Penguin Group (USA), a Pearson
company, exclusively for Dolly Parton's Imagination Library, a not-for-profit
program designed to inspire a love of reading and learning, sponsored in part by The
Dollywood Foundation. Penguin's trade editions of this work are available wherever
books are sold.

$\mathcal{E}$ach and every moment
of each and every day,
amazing things are happening. . . .

The moment you are waking up
from a good-night's sleep,
somewhere in the early light
there's a band of sheep
following their leader,
walking in a line,
on a steep and narrow trail
along a mountain spine.

You wash your face and comb your hair
and brush and floss your teeth,

and as you do, a toothy shark
is circling a reef.

At that exact same moment
in the Arctic, cold and white,

a polar bear is running fast
across a field of ice.

And in a fragrant meadow
on a green and grassy hill,
a mother bear rolls on her side
to feed her cubs bear milk.

Every moment of your day
is matched by other moments
near and far away.

You take a sip of water
from the fountain in your school,
and someplace in the forest
a deer drinks from a pool.

In the middle of the afternoon
when where you are is hot,
the temperature keeps rising
but you wish that it did not.

At that very moment
in the desert, there's an owl
who's found a perfect place to hide—
a cactus hole way up high
and nice and cool inside.

While on the cool and breezy coast
beside a fishing boat,

a finback whale is surfacing
right where a white gull floats.

And not far from the whale and gull
on an island in the fog,

a herd of seals are resting
on rocks and driftwood logs.

At your dinner table,
you heap food upon your dish.
And on a cliff beside the ocean,
puffins dine on fresh-caught fish.

An owl swoops down to catch a rat.
A beaver gnaws a tree.

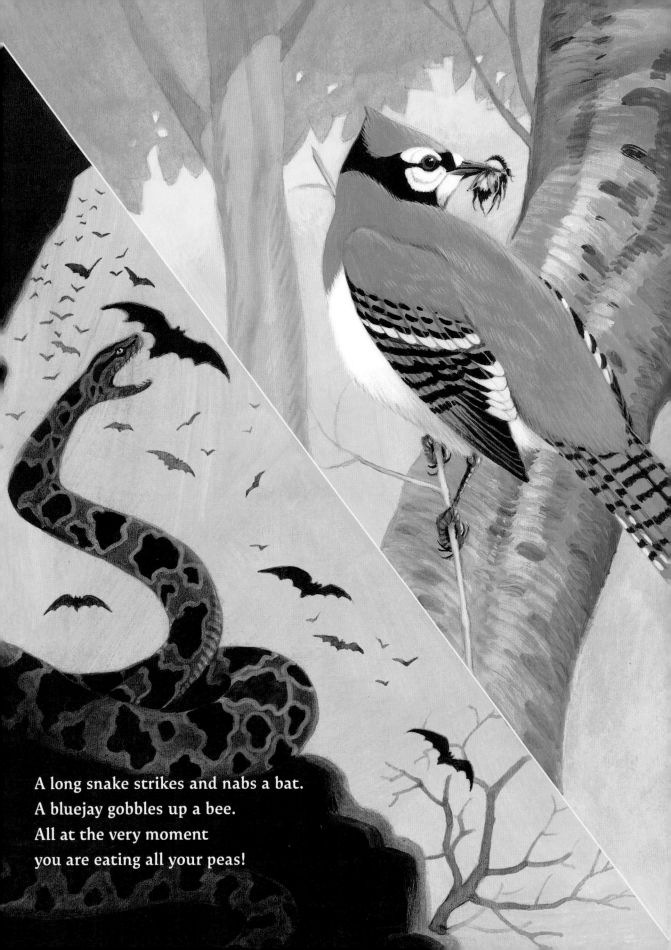

A long snake strikes and nabs a bat.
A bluejay gobbles up a bee.
All at the very moment
you are eating all your peas!

After finishing your homework,
you take some time to sketch
an alligator sunning
along the water's edge.

And as you add big pointed teeth
to the gator that you draw,
a real alligator somewhere
is opening its jaws.

At bedtime when your room
is as quiet as can be,
think of all the wild things
far and near that you don't see.

Pretend you're hearing lions
roaring in the dark.
Or try to guess what squirrels dream,
sleeping in the park.

Picture raccoons coming out to hunt,
blackbirds taking flight,
and a pair of pelicans
flying in to roost all night.

Think of all the animals
getting sleepy, too,
who at this very moment
will fall asleep with you.

Notes on Animals

The animals I thought about while writing this book were, in some cases, a world away from my Vermont farm. But I have seen most of them in the wild, and whenever I think of them I am transported momentarily to their part of the world. And I become aware again that my life is happening simultaneously to theirs. Just knowing this makes me care more about wild places and wild things. I encourage this sort of daydreaming.

Here are a few notes about the animals I daydreamed about while working on this book:

The ROCKY MOUNTAIN SHEEP are like ones my wife, Deanna, and I saw as they traversed a steep cliffside just outside of Deadwood, South Dakota.

The BLACKTIP SHARK is one of the types of reef sharks we look for and look out for off the Florida Keys. There are POLAR BEARS just 500 miles north of Vermont. Someday I hope to travel to James Bay to see them in the wild. I think about them often and can easily picture them running on the ice.

The BLACK BEAR and her cinnamon-colored cubs were seen and photographed in Yellowstone by a good friend of mine. We have quite a few black bears in the forest around us, and I think about them every time I walk in our woods.

The WHITE-TAILED DEER was on Assateague Island. After it drank, it swam in the water.

The ELF OWL lives in the Sonoran Desert. They don't make the holes in the saguaro cactus. Woodpeckers do. But the owls make good use of them.

The FINBACK WHALE rose in the Atlantic Ocean one foggy Maine afternoon and gave Deanna and me a sight we'll remember forever. The HARBOR and GRAY SEALS were congregated not far away.

The PUFFINS live on a protected Maine island
where, if you have a good boat, you can see them
fish for food and raise their young.

BARN OWLS are owls of farm fields and wooded edges.
The BEAVER is a neighbor of ours, as is the BLUE JAY. But the
SNAKE is one I imagined after hearing that if a snake is long enough,
it can catch bats as they exit or enter a cave.

Because we love being in the Everglades, we see our
share of ALLIGATORS. And I think about them in
their subtropical world nearly every day of the year.

The LIONS are in my dreams.

The RACCOONS are in my woodshed.

And my favorite bird, the BROWN PELICAN, is always
in my heart.

Jim Arnosky